First edition March 2015
Published by Crewman #4 Productions LLC

Printed in the United States of America

ISBN 978-0-9864262-0-9

ABLE SEAMAN

Just Nuisance

Written by Sherri Rowe
Illustrations by Alex Zandria

Dedicated to the memory of

all the sailors who gave their

lives in service of their country...

For all those good and faithful

friends who remind us daily to

be humble, kind, and giving...

...and mostly to

Able Seaman

Just Nuisance.

We discovered the story of Just Nuisance while enjoying a working holiday in South Africa. A friend who lived in Cape Town suggested we visit a sleepy naval village along the Cape coast called Simon's Town. Our friend directed us to the famous African Penguins who live in this lovely village and encouraged us to explore the charming seaside home of the South African Navy. In addition, we visited Cape Point, with the delightful Cape Point Lighthouse, and the Cape of Good Hope located right around the corner.

We stopped to explore the central portion of downtown Simon's Town called Jubilee Square. Located in the heart of this quaint village, the square and the neighboring area harkens back to an almost forgotten romantic era filled with gallant gentlemen and heroes from the past. In fact, many of the surrounding buildings have changed very little in the past hundred years.

This enchanting, tree-lined area is surrounded by unique shops overflowing with handmade goods from around Africa, as well as local restaurants filled with enticing aromas. Unlike the scintillating chaos of the world-famous Greenmarket Square in downtown Cape Town, this little market, while teeming with eager vendors hawking their goods, retained a quiet dignity.

As we wandered around the square we encountered a bronze statue of a very large Great Dane. The attached placard identified the dog as JUST NUISANCE. Unfortunately there was frustratingly little other information so we returned to a nearby shop to make our inquires. We were directed to the Simon's Town Museum and were told it was within walking distance of the statue. After a fortuitous detour into and through the intriguing South African Naval Museum, we found our way down the street and eventually discovered the home of all things Just Nuisance. A delightful house tucked down a winding path overlooking the crystal bay, a fitting repository to the story of our heroic pooch. Here we began our journey with the wonderful staff of the museum and our four-legged friend. We hope you enjoy his story as much as we do…

- *Sherri Rowe*

Life-size bronze statue of Just Nuisance

Jubilee Square

Simon's Town, South Africa

Just Nuisance was born on the 1st of April 1937 in Rondebosch, South Africa. At that time, Rondebosch was a sleepy little hamlet nestled in the hills between Cape Town and Simon's Town at the far southern end of the continent of Africa. Today it is considered a suburb of Cape Town, but back then it was a tiny gem hidden far from the hustle and bustle of the big city.

The year Nuisance was born, South Africa was a colony of the British Empire and the world was on the brink of war. However, the insanity that had begun to grip Europe seemed a long way away. But soon this little corner of the world would become an important link in the South Atlantic Theatre of Operations during World War II. Simon's Town was the home of HMS *Afrikander*, the naval station located along False Bay. The base was also home to an enormous and invaluable dry dock, large enough to accommodate the necessary repairs of warships. Simon's Town would soon be sleepy no more.

However, on this day, in this little part of the world, the only news of any significance was a large litter of puppies had been born to two purebred Great Danes named Diana and Koning. One of the puppies was registered as *The Pride of* Rondebosch with the South African Kennel Union. Although we do not know what his owner called him at the time, this puppy would one day earn the name Just Nuisance and become a legend on two continents. Mr. Bosman was the original owner of these Great Dan puppies. He was a kind and loving owner and he wanted to find the perfect homes for his special puppies so he put an ad in the local papers.

Cape Town • Simon's Town

All the adorable puppies quickly found homes except one. This puppy was big. He was much bigger than his littermates, curious and intelligent. Soon he was the only one left. The lonely pup continued to outgrow and outweigh even the largest of Great Danes. This breed is typically very large, but Just Nuisance was massive from birth and just kept getting bigger. Fully grown, he was over six feet tall when standing on his hind legs. He was 150 pounds of bone and muscle and Mr. Bosman needed to find a place where Just Nuisance could run and play.

Just Nuisance with his mates

When he was eleven months old, Just Nuisance finally found a home as the dearly beloved pet of Mr. Benjamin Chaney who lived in the Cape Town suburb of Mowbray. Mr. Chaney had lost his Bullmastiff, another very large breed of dog, and was looking for a new companion. He found the ad in the newspaper offering a large Great Dane for sale. The gigantic dog was an ideal replacement for the dog he had just lost. It was a perfect fit. Just Nuisance loved his new family and they loved him.

The first day in his new home, his owner showed Just Nuisance around the house and yard. Nuisance loved his new quarters and seemed to understand immediately that this was his domain. While in the back yard, Just Nuisance decided it was time to do his "business". He picked a spot out of sight, carefully covered his work, and returned to Mr. Chaney to shake his hand. This was a lifelong pattern for Nuisance and he always conducted himself politely and accordingly.

Mr. Chaney decided he wanted a sandwich so he went back inside and into the kitchen. Just Nuisance trailed along, watching every move of his new owner. Nuisance sat down and studied Mr. Chaney as he opened the refrigerator door, removed a large roast mutton and sliced himself a piece to make a sandwich. Just Nuisance stared up longingly until his new friend lopped off a fist-size chunk and tossed it to the eager hound. Just Nuisance gulped and swallowed the morsel whole, eagerly looking around for more.

The following morning Chaney, along with his wife, meandered into the kitchen to fix breakfast. As they entered, they noticed the refrigerator door was standing wide open. An empty plate sat on the bottom shelf and the roast mutton was nowhere to be found. In the middle of the kitchen floor, they discovered a snoring Just Nuisance peacefully guarding his mutton bone.

It was not long before Mr. Chaney realized his massive dog was going to eat them out of house and home. Alternative arrangements had to be made and soon Nuisance was looking for a new home once again.

Shortly after making Just Nuisance a part of the family, Mr. Chaney was placed in charge of the Simon's Town United Services' Institute. The Institute offered a place to stay, refreshments, and general comfort to all servicemen of the Royal Navy, Army and Air Force. This provided the perfect opportunity to remove Nuisance from the home but keep him as part of the family.

Just Nuisance went with his friend to act as guard dog. Due to the proximity of the Simon's Town Naval Station, the Institute was always full of sailors. It was here that our furry friend formed his life-long affinity for the men of the sea. He was especially fond of the men who wore the square rig of enlisted seamen. No one really knows why he preferred the enlisted ranks over officers, but he always treated them quite differently.

Perhaps it had something to do with a visit by HMS *Neptune* and their dog-loving crew. It was these sailors who gave our precocious pooch his unique name. One bright and sunny afternoon HMS *Neptune* came alongside Simon's Town to resupply. The sailors met Nuisance on the dock and immediately bonded with the friendly dog. Nuisance, recognizing his mates, and probably looking for a handout, followed the sailors aboard their ship.

WWII poster promoting the Empire working together for victory

This was no small thing because, although he would one day become a dutiful member of the Royal Navy, he absolutely hated water. Nevertheless, this is how he began his naval career and how he acquired his name.

On that fateful day, Just Nuisance decided he was most comfortable lying lengthwise *across* the busiest gangway accessing the ship. Every time a sailor had to enter or leave the ship in the execution of his duties, he had to maneuver his way around the enormous dog. It was a gigantic nuisance. And, while all the sailors were terribly fond of the dog, they were sailors, and they expressed their displeasure by calling him names. When it came time to officially name him, they simply labeled him as they knew him: Nuisance, just a nuisance...and the legend was born.

HMS *Neptune* leaves Simon's Town

Around this time Just Nuisance began to follow the particularly generous chief petty officer (CPO) steward of HMS *Neptune* into Cape Town on the train. The gigantic dog had been regularly fed by this CPO from the food stores of the ship. Just Nuisance was a very smart dog and he knew a good thing when he had it so he stuck close to his new friend. The big-hearted man always paid for a ticket for the dog to ride the train. While the ticket collectors tolerated the riding of the dog on their exalted railway, they did not like it. Just Nuisance took up three seats and even though his ticket had been paid for, he was allocated only one.

Just Nuisance rides on the South African Railways

It did not take long for Just Nuisance to figure out there was many a meal at the end of the Simon's Town to Cape Town run. Sailors are generous by nature and they always stood Nuisance a pint or two. Unfortunately, often times those same sailors who paid for his ticket into town did not pay for his ticket home. The South African Railways was not happy with the freeloading dog.

By now, Just Nuisance was one of the crew. He followed his sailors from place to place, enjoying everything the sailors enjoyed. He was particularly fond of meat pies and loved a little nip with his buddies. He was known to tipple a bit too much and often times ended his night on the town in the Royal Naval Hospital where he was watched over by doctors and nurses until he recovered.

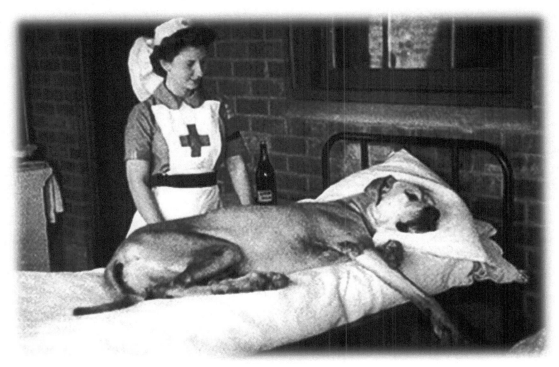

Just Nuisance under the watchful eye of a loving nurse

Y ou see Just Nuisance was no ordinary dog. Prior to the last train leaving Cape Town, he would go around to the dockside pubs and bark at the sailors until they got the message and left for the station. He always knew when the last train was leaving. How he knew we will never know, but he always made sure his mates were safe and sound aboard the final train home.

Everyone loved him. Well almost everyone, but it was not just for his good looks and charm. Just Nuisance was keenly intelligent and many a night he patrolled through each train car making certain every sailor had disembarked and was safely on the way to his bed in Simon's Town. No sailor was ever AWOL, sailor lingo for *absent without leave*, while Just Nuisance was on watch.

This desire to be with his mates at all times contributed to his ongoing battle with the South African Railways. Nuisance was big and he was, well, a nuisance. He sprawled across three seats and was very intimidating to those who did not know him. Complaints were filed by civilians who resented sharing their train ride with a dog. While their complaints were perhaps justified, Just Nuisance was no ordinary dog. He took the animosity of his fellow travelers in stride by simply ignoring them. In the case of the conductor on the regular route from Simon's Town to Cape Town, Nuisance simply chose to tolerate him.

Occasionally, this conductor would put Just Nuisance off at one of the stations between Simon's Town and Cape Town. Nuisance usually tolerated this and would simply wait on the platform for the next train going to Cape Town and get on. He was frequently observed looking at the posted timetables, seemingly reading the train schedule. As far as anyone can tell, he always got on the right train.

One time, for reasons unknown, Nuisance decided he would tolerate removal from the train no longer. This time, when the conductor tried to put him off, Nuisance put the conductor off instead. This confrontation escalated the battle with the South African Railways to full-fledged war.

Just Nuisance did not like it when his mates would get into fights. If he saw sailors fighting, he would physically get between them to break it up, barking as if to say, "You know better than that...cut it out."

If necessary he would use his massive jaws to grab an errant arm or leg to "encourage" the combatants to cease and desist. He knew precisely how much pressure to use and never broke the skin of any sailor. Even though our canny canine was strong enough to seriously harm a human, there is no record of him ever doing so.

Nuisance had a very special relationship with the sailors who put in at Simon's Town but he would not tolerate insubordination among the ranks. He monitored the behavior of his sailor buddies with admirable consistency. He was, however, not so strict with himself and there are a number of minor infractions listed in his service record.

Just Nuisance with his puppies appears in the local paper

Sailors often tell fantastic tales and over the years the stories grow to unbelievable proportions. This certainly might be the case with some of the stories told about Just Nuisance, but there are a number of well-documented tales of heroism that show his loyalty, devotion, and intelligence.

Just Nuisance was strolling down a street in Cape Town one evening when he heard shouting and scuffling down an alley. He quickly went to investigate, scared off the attackers, and discovered a sailor bleeding from a stab wound. He immediately sprang into action. He ran back down the alley, barking like a lunatic trying to get attention from anyone who would listen. He found a taxi driver lounging in his cab. With his frantic actions, Nuisance convinced him to follow along.

The taxi driver saw the injured sailor, quickly summoned an ambulance and the sailor was saved. If Just Nuisance had not come along when he did, and known what to do, the sailor might have died.

Just Nuisance was a hero to many but not to everyone. The South African Railways disliked him with a deep passion because he loved to ride on their trains. Frequently sailors, civilians, or total strangers would pay the train fare for Nuisance to ride into town. Equally often, however, he would simply get on the next available train to Cape Town, unaccompanied and unpaid. It did not help that he liked to ride in the first-class carriage and frequently disrupted other passengers. A few complaints were filed against the railway-riding rascal and the South African Railways used that as an excuse to take action.

PROCLAMATION
of the
SOUTH AFRICAN RAILWAYS

REWARD

THIS DOG HAS BEEN DECLARED A

NUISANCE

CONTACT SOUTH AFRICAN RAILWAYS WITH INFORMATION LEADING TO HIS CAPTURE TO COLLECT THE REWARD

They issued what could effectively be called a death warrant. Mr. Chaney was told that if his delinquent dog could not be kept off the trains, the South African Railways would capture and destroy him. Chaney knew he could not guarantee that the free-spirited dog would not ride the rails, so he decided he would have to sell Just Nuisance to keep him away from the trains. With a heavy heart, he pledged to give the proceeds of the sale to the *Speed the Planes* fund.

HMS AFRIKANDER
SIMON'S TOWN, SOUTH AFRICA

Thousands of letters and telegrams arrived in protest to the threatened destruction of Just Nuisance

Word of the threatened destruction of their beloved mate quickly spread throughout the Simon's Town area. Sailors of all ranks and civilians up and down the Cape Peninsula raised such an outcry it was heard as far away as London. The Commander in Chief (C-in-C) South Atlantic Station was deluged with letters of protest and concern about Just Nuisance. Thousands of letters and telegrams arrived urging the C-in-C to act and do something to save their adored mascot. Bags of letters were also delivered to the Admiral's office in Simon's Town. The locals, as well as the sailors, had fallen in love with Just Nuisance and they were frantic to save him.

What followed was an act unprecedented in the history of British naval operations. The C-in-C, South Atlantic Station, issued a decree that Just Nuisance was to become an official member of His Majesty's Navy. Orders were sent to HMS *Afrikander* in Simon's Town advising that Just Nuisance was to be enlisted as a volunteer in His Majesty's Navy. As such, he was to be "afforded all the privileges accordingly due". This act would save Nuisance from the evil clutches of the South African Railways, as all military personnel in uniform could ride on the railway for free.

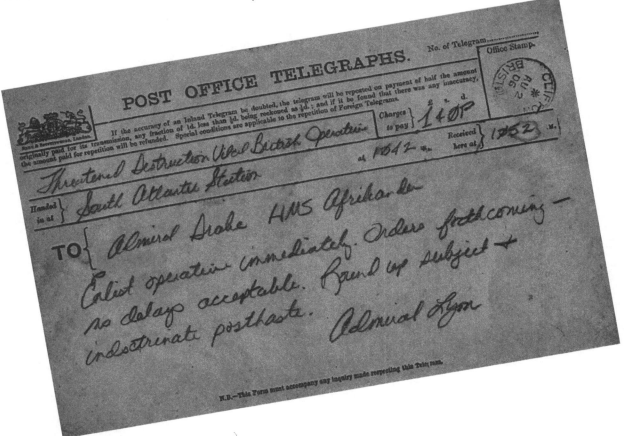

While Just Nuisance was busy fighting with the South African Railways, Mr. Chaney was busy buying another dog. This time he chose a happy, floppy bulldog he named Ajax. Just Nuisance tolerated him as long as the interloper did not try to enter the United Services Institute. If Ajax did not interfere with the relationship between Nuisance and his sailors, everything was fine, and the daffy dog seemed to have understood this relationship. Just Nuisance even protected Ajax and would bark and snarl ferociously if anyone attempted to pick on his pudgy pal.

On occasion, Nuisance would allow Ajax to accompany him into Cape Town for a night on the town. His loyal companion would merrily trot to the station where he would try to heave his short, stocky body onto the train. Unfortunately there was a great distance between the platform and the doorway to the train carriage. Just Nuisance would let Ajax struggle for a bit and then put his large nose under the tail end of his little buddy and shove him onto the train. Then Nuisance would carefully grab the portly pup by the scruff of his neck and hoist him up to share his seat.

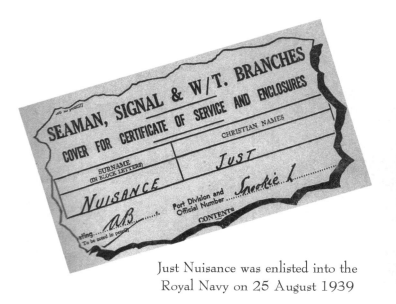

Just Nuisance was enlisted into the
Royal Navy on 25 August 1939

Finally the big day arrived. Hundreds of locals and sailors gathered for the ceremony and on 25 August 1939, Just Nuisance was inducted into the Royal Navy. He remains, to this day, the only canine ever officially enlisted into the British Navy. After his enlistment, he was accorded all the privileges of his human counterparts, including a pay packet, rum ration and his personal favorite, full meal privileges. He ate when his mates ate, and was provided fresh cream milk, meat, and bones for every meal. He did not have to eat any fruits or vegetables and was served his favorite dessert, Spotted Dick pudding, a popular British custard made with dried fruit, at almost every dinner. But, he had responsibilities too and he took them seriously.

CERTIFICATE of the Service of

SURNAME (IN BLACK LETTERS)	CHRISTIAN NAME OR NAMES
Nuisance	Just (Alias - Pride of Rondebosch)

in the Royal Navy.

NOTE.—The corner of this Certificate is to be cut off where indicated, if the man is discharged with a "Bad" character or with disgrace, or if specially directed by the Admiralty. If the corner is cut off, the fact is to be noted in the Ledger.

Port Division	Snookie.	Man's Signature on discharge to Pension	
Official No.	One		
Date of Birth	1st. April 1937.	Nearest known Relative or Friend (To be noted in pencil).	
Where born { Parish	Rondebosch.	Relationship	
		Name.	
Town or County	C.P.	Address	
Trade brought up to	Bonecrusher.	Stre - Kountry.	
Religious Denomination	Scrounger.	Dam - Diana.	

All Engagements, including Non-C.S., to be noted in these Columns.			Swimming Qualifications.		
Date of actually volunteering	Commencement of time	Period volunteered for	Date	Qualification	Signature
1. 6 June '39	25 Aug 39	Period of the	1. 30 Sep 39	P.P.T. (V.G.)	
2.		present	2.		
3.		emergency.	3.		
4.			4.		
5.			5.		
6.			6.		

Certificate of Service Just Nuisance

Just Nuisance was duly sworn in and his right paw was pressed onto the inkpad and then pressed onto the place where his signature would have gone. He was given a disc with his name, rank, and official number just like all ratings in the Royal Navy, along with a collar with a brass plate. The brass plate carried the words *South African Railways, Free Pass*. Nuisance did not like his new collar, even though it gave him the freedom he desired, and disliked even more his new hat and cap tally. He was frequently seen out of uniform and eventually he was officially excused from wearing his cap altogether.

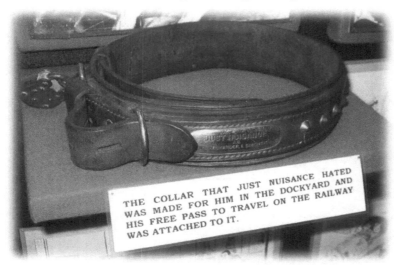

THE COLLAR THAT JUST NUISANCE HATED WAS MADE FOR HIM IN THE DOCKYARD AND HIS FREE PASS TO TRAVEL ON THE RAILWAY WAS ATTACHED TO IT.

This is the actual collar of Just Nuisance on display at the Simon's Town Museum

Just Nuisance was assigned to HMS *Afrikander* and billeted at a small naval base called Froggy Pond located about five miles from Simon's Town. It was thought Nuisance would get into less trouble away from the docks, but nothing could have been further from the truth. Just Nuisance was assigned the "dog watches", and while he frequently caused chaos, he performed his duties very earnestly.

Nuisance was also issued an official mattress along with a pillow, sheets, and a blanket for his own personal bunk. He took his privileges very seriously and made sure everyone understood his position. One evening Nuisance came into the barracks to find a sailor had mistakenly fallen asleep in his bunk. Just Nuisance pushed the sleeping sailor off his bunk and onto the floor. The sailor bounced up off the floor ready for a fight. Just Nuisance simply pushed him down again, snorted into the air as if to say that was the end of that, and turned to get into bed. The ensuing argument became legendary throughout the Cape Peninsula, ending in victory for Nuisance and an apology from the errant sailor. Nuisance gracefully accepted the apology and promptly went to bed.

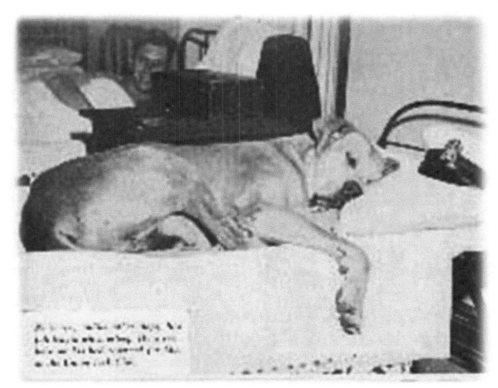

Just Nuisance appeared in numerous magazines, often to benefit fundraising efforts for the war

There is no doubt Just Nuisance was a very large dog who would not tolerate shenanigans from his human pals. He was, however, very affectionate with children. If he accidently bumped into one of the smaller members of the human kind, he would politely and gently offer his paw to be shaken as a gesture of goodwill. That is, of course, unless you happened to be sitting in the seat he wanted on the train.

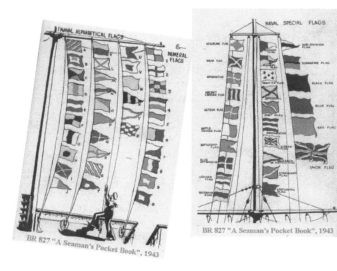

Signal flag instruction page from "Seaman's Pocket Book 1943"

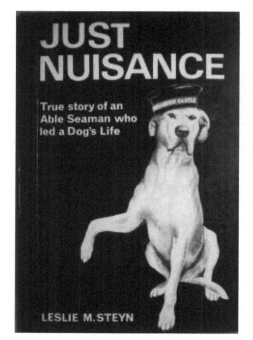

Just Nuisance stories sold to raise funds for the war effort

One time, Nuisance spied three young girls sitting on what he clearly considered his seat. He gently placed his backside on the edge of their seat and carefully maneuvered himself back and forth until the three young girls were soundly deposited on the train floor. He offered his paw as if to say, "We should remain friends in spite of your misguided use of my seat." The girls accepted his peace offering and giggled on their way to another seat, happy to have had the opportunity to interact with the famous dog.

There are hundreds of stories about Just Nuisance and his time as an Able Seaman in the Royal Navy. Almost all of them show how keenly intelligent and exceptionally loyal he was to his sailor mates.

Although he generally avoided women, one story tells of how Nuisance decided to dance a waltz with a young lady. He invited her to dance by barking and placing his massive paws on her shoulders. He then proceeded to dance in correct time to a traditional waltz.

Another story has him flying as a frequent passenger in a Fairey Battle light bomber from Royal Naval Air Station Wingfield. Even though dogs were not allowed in military planes, Nuisance loved to fly and frequently flew with a pilot who risked his career to take him up.

Just Nuisance
Royal Naval Air Station Wingfield

One of his favorite places to visit was the Texas Bar in Cape Town. Perhaps he liked it best because it had batwing doors, like an Old West saloon, and he could enter and leave as he desired. The Texas Bar also had a wonderful balcony on the second floor. Nuisance liked to lean on the railings and look down on the people passing by. It was here he was treated to his favorite meat pies and lager. He

was so intelligent he even learned to moderate his drinking so he would not feel so miserable the next morning.

One evening he went with his mates to the local dance hall and witnessed dancers perform for the first time. Apparently, he was not fond of the performance and decided to visit his special brand of chaos onto the stage. He chased the dancing girls around until they ran screaming from the building. He then sat back down and finished his pint.

He was dognapped once by the members of a visiting British County Class cruiser. The crew, like almost everyone who met Just Nuisance, fell in love with him and decided to smuggle him on board. After the ship had sailed, Nuisance slipped his hijackers and made for the rails. He leapt over and swam to shore.

Nuisance loved the sound of the *"fluitjie"* or mouth organ. He would sit and listen for hours, unless the sailor played the British National Anthem too many times. The playing of the national anthem necessitated standing to attention. He dutifully stood to attention every time the anthem was played but could tolerate doing this only so many times in a row.

The loveable pup never forgot a kindness or service given to him. He once had a large in-grown toenail that was removed by the base Surgeon-Commander. Nuisance was tremendously grateful and for the rest of his life, whenever he saw that particular doctor, he stopped and offered his paw for a thank you shake.

World War II Victory Posters

One of his most endearing habits seemed to have started quite by accident. One evening, coming home on the train from a night on the town, Nuisance awoke to discover the ticket collector trying to wake up the sailors who had partaken of too much tipple and were still asleep in their seats.

Just Nuisance went from compartment to compartment assisting the conductor in waking up his errant mates. He would grab them by the sleeve and pull

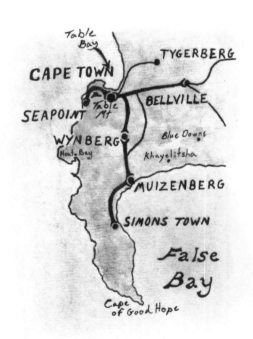

them to the floor. This would usually wake them up to send them on their way, but some just groaned and went back to sleep. Here Nuisance showed his uncanny intelligence once again as he hopped off the train, ran to his mates who were already headed back to base, grabbed one by the cuff and dragged him back to the train. He barked at the sleeping sailors indicating they needed help and the sailor got the message.

The sailor yelled to his buddies for help and they dragged, carried, and cajoled every sailor safely back to their barracks. Nuisance repeated this performance every single time he caught the last train to Simon's Town. There is no doubt; Just Nuisance saved many a sailor from being adrift.

This was one of the many reasons the sailors loved Just Nuisance.

Just Nuisance found his fame came in handy for fundraising events. He was often invited to festivities across the Cape and would travel with the Commanding Officer to carefully chosen parties. Nuisance enjoyed his time in the spotlight but he did not have a great track record with other dogs. Therefore, everyone

First Day Cover issued in 1994

was instructed to make certain all dogs were secured before his arrival. Things went well for a while until a fateful garden party where a small Pekinese got loose. Our courageous canine felt obliged to chase the little varmint through the tent, over the food tables and into the punch bowl. As a result of this disaster, Nuisance was excused from future fundraisers.

He did however lend his likeness to fundraising postcards, stories, and less formal events, such as Boy Scout rallies.

Fundraising postcard celebrating the "marriage" of Just Nuisance and Adinda

Just Nuisance meets his puppies

He also found time to get married to the Great Dane, Adinda, at Hout Bay in June of 1941, and sire five puppies. Two, named Victor and Wilhelmina, were auctioned off and the proceeds were given to the war effort.

There are many stories about Just Nuisance. Some are tall tales that have grown throughout the decades. The ones that seem the most outrageous are most likely the truth.

We know that Just Nuisance saved lives on more than one occasion. He once sounded the alarm for a sailor who had passed out in the back of a little-used building. The sailor had just arrived in Simon's Town on a ship that had recently called in at Sierra Leone. There, he had unknowingly contracted malaria. If Nuisance had not found him and demanded by his actions the medical attention needed, the sailor could have died.

There is no doubt that Just Nuisance touched the lives of many in ways both large and small.

Just Nuisance aboard with the sailors he loved

37

A picture of Nuisance was carried by a fellow Able Seaman throughout his internment in a Japanese prisoner-of-war camp after his ship, HMS *Encounter*, was sunk in enemy action in the Java Sea. The picture meant so much to the sailor that he risked severe punishment to keep it.

There have been numerous songs and poems written about Just Nuisance. Throughout the years, books and pamphlets chronicling his exploits have been published and distributed around the world. It is a testament to the affect he had on those who knew him that his legacy lives on even today.

Greetings, shipmate! This picture of Just Nuisance, taken on board the destroyer HMS Encounter at Simon's Town, was buried in the ground or hidden elsewhere with other personal belongings of Able Seaman Ray Stubbs of Newbury, Berkshire, in Japanese POW camps in Sumatra after Encounter was sunk by enemy action in the Java Sea.

Just Nuisance touched the lives of innumerable sailors the world over. Often their time with him was brief but sometimes they had the opportunity to bond more deeply. The more time a sailor had with the loveable mutt, the harder it was to say good bye. Often times sailors would request a private moment with Just Nuisance and it seemed as if the uncanny dog understood the need for a special good bye.

One sailor said his farewells and attempted to dry his eyes without anyone noticing. As he turned away from his friend one final time, Nuisance barked. It seemed as if he was saying, "I will never forget you either."

And, for generations after World War II, in pubs around the globe, someone would mention they had put in at Simon's Town and immediately the conversation would turn to stories of Just Nuisance.

Those generations are passing into the night, but the story of Just Nuisance lives on. He will always be remembered for what he stood for and what he represented – the very best, most loyal, friendship "humanly" possible.

A moment of relaxation for a sailor and Just Nuisance

EPILOGUE

Great Danes do not live to a grand old age under the best of circumstances. Just Nuisance had lived hard and played even harder. He loved to ride in the trucks with his mates, but whenever he decided he wanted to get off, he would simply jump. Most of the time all would be well, but on a couple of occasions he was seriously hurt. As the result of a particularly bad accident, paralysis began to take over his hindquarters. The veterinary surgeon said there was nothing that could be done.

On 1 April 1944, the day of his seventh birthday, his companions took him by truck to the Royal Naval Hospital in Simon's Town. Just Nuisance seemed to understand that he was going on his last ride. It appeared as if he was actually trying to cheer up his mates, as if to say, "It's okay boys, I understand."

The Naval Surgeon put Nuisance to sleep that day and a great friend and companion left this world.

On 2 April 1944 at 11:30 a.m. his body was wrapped in a canvas bag and covered with a white Royal Naval Ensign. Able Seaman Just Nuisance R.N. was then laid to rest with full military honors at Klaver Camp at the top of Red Hill. A party of Royal Marines fired a farewell salute and a lone bugler played *The Last Post*. The ceremony was attended by many and even the strongest of men shed a tear as they said goodbye to their dearly beloved friend. Just Nuisance sleeps peacefully for all time high above the Simon's Town Naval Station overlooking the sailors he loved so very much.

A simple granite gravestone stands guard at the head of his last resting place and can still be visited today in Simon's Town, South Africa.

ACKNOWLEDGMENTS

I would like to extend a special thank you to Cathrynne Salter-Jansen for her unfailing support of this project. A big thank you to everyone at the Simon's Town Museum and especially the Friends of the Simon's Town Museum for their encouragement and support. They love the silly dog even more than we do.

Thank you to the Marquardt family and to John Dorrington. I am humbled by your friendship. Thank you to Glenn von Zeil and Admiral Arne Söderlund, you both know how important you are to the success of this endeavor.

I would also like to take this opportunity to thank the staff of the Simon's Town Museum; Margaret Constant, Nontlalontle (Vicky) Mlanjeni, Buyiswa (Maria) Ponti, and Suzette Farmer; as well as The Board of Trustees.

And finally, we would like to extend our love and devotion to all the incredible South Africans we are honored to call friends. South Africa is one of the most wonderful places on earth, filled with some of the most wonderful people on earth. It is a hidden gem, glittering in the crystal blue oceans which surround it.

Profits from the book benefit the Friends of Simon's Town Museum

Simon's Town Museum
The Residency
Court Road
Simon's Town
7995 South Africa
Curator: Cathy Salter-Jansen
Phone: +27 21 786 3046
Email: cathy@simonstownmuseum.co.za
Website: http://simonstown.com/museum/stm.htm
(Take the first left turn after the Simon's Town Railway Station)

South African Naval Museum
Curator: CDR Leon Steyn
Dockyard Magazine, Church and Store-house,
Naval Dockyard
St Georges Street
Private Bag X1
Simon's Town
7995, South Africa
Phone: +27 21 787 4686
Phone: +27 21 787 4635
Email: leonsteyn70@gmail.com
Website: http://www.simonstown.com/navalmuseum/

Simon's Town Boat Company
Dave Hurwitz
The Town Pier
Wharf Street
Simon's Town
7975, South Africa
Phone: +27 83 257 7760
Fax: +27 21 786 3216
Email: info@boatcompany.co.za
Website: http://boatcompany.co.za/

SAS Assegaai - S99 Submarine Museum
The South African Naval Museum
Manager: Rear Admiral (JG) Arne Soderlund SAN (Ret)
Bookings: +27 21 786 5243
Email: s99@sanavy.co.za or info@hgtstours.com
Website: http://www.navy.mil.za/museum_submarine/
Pick-up point at Jubilee Square (113 St Georges Street, Simon's Town)

All photographs are from the archives, displays and media of the Simon's Town Museum, Simon's Town, South Africa and used with permission, unless otherwise stated.

Page 5, 6, 36:	Private Collection of Sherri Rowe
Page 10:	Photo used with kind permission of John McGregor, OBE Commander Retired HNS Neptune Association
Page 22, 34, 37:	Private Collection of James Bisbey
Page 34, 35, 36:	Private Collection of Bruce Bisbey
Back Cover:	Private Collections of James Bisbey, Bruce Bisbey & Sherri Rowe

COMING SOON

...to a theatre near you!

Support the movie Just Nuisance at
justnuisancethemovie.com
like us on FACEBOOK Justnuisancethemovie
follow us on Twitter @JNTheMovie
blog at JustNuisanceAbleSeaman.blogspot.com
or email us at
able.seaman.just.nuisance.ddp @ gmail.com